The Wiley COBOL Syntax Reference Guide: With IBM and VAX Enhancements

Prepared by
NANCY STERN and ROBERT A. STERN

The following acknowledgment has been reproduced from COBOL Edition, U.S. Department of Defense, at the request of the Conference on Data Systems Languages.

"Any organization interested in reproducing the COBOL report and specifications in whole or in part, using ideas taken from this report as the basis for an instruction manual or for any other purpose is free to do so. However, all such organizations are requested to reproduce this section as part of the introduction to the document. Those using a short passage, as in a book review, are requested to mention 'COBOL' in acknowledgment of the source, but need not quote this entire section.

"COBOL is an industry language and is not the property of any company or group of companies, or of any organization or group of organizations.

"No warranty, expressed or implied, is made by any contributor or by the COBOL Committee as to the accuracy and functioning of the programming system and language. Moreover, no responsibility is assumed by any contributor or by the committee, in connection therewith.

"Procedures have been established for the maintenance of COBOL. Inquiries concerning the procedures for proposing changes should be directed to the Executive Committee of the Conference on Data Systems Languages.

"The authors and copyright holders of the copyrighted material used herein

FLOW-MATIC (Trademark of Sperry Rand Corporation), Programming for the Univac (R) I and II, Data Automation Systems copyrighted 1958, 1959, by Sperry Rand Corporation; IBM Commercial Translator Form No. F28-8013, copyrighted 1959 by IBM; FACT, DSI 27A5260-2760, copyrighted 1960 by Minneapolis-Honeywell

have specifically authorized the use of this material in whole or in part, in the COBOL specifications. Such authorization extends to the reproduction and use of COBOL specifications in programming manuals or similar publications."

CONTENTS

COBOL Syntax Reference Guide

I. COBOL Character Set

The following lists are in ascending order:

EBCDIC		ASCII	
	space		space
.	period, decimal point	"	quotation mark
<	less than	$	dollar sign
(	left parenthesis	'	single quotation mark
+	plus symbol	(	left parenthesis
$	dollar sign	)	right parenthesis

*	asterisk, multiplication	*	asterisk, multiplication
)	right parenthesis	+	plus symbol
;	semicolon	,	comma
-	hyphen, minus sign	-	hyphen, minus sign
/	slash, division	.	period, decimal point
,	comma	/	slash, division
>	greater than	0–9	digits
'	single quotation mark	;	semicolon
=	equal sign	<	less than
"	quotation mark	=	equal sign
a–z	lowercase letters	>	greater than
A–Z	uppercase letters	A–Z	uppercase letters
0–9	digits	a–z	lowercase letters

II. COBOL Reserved Words

Each COBOL compiler has a list of reserved words that:

1. Includes all entries in the ANS COBOL standard.
2. Includes additional entries not part of the standard but that are either VAX or IBM compiler extensions. These are called enhancements.

The following is based on the 1974 and 1985 American National Standard. You may find that your computer has additional reserved words. Diagnostic messages will print if you are using a reserved word incorrectly.

New reserved words that are not relevant for COBOL 74, but are relevant only for COBOL 85, are denoted with a single asterisk (*). COBOL 74 reserved words that are *not* reserved in the new standard are denoted with a double asterisk (**). Words in red are VAX COBOL 85 extensions. Words in blue are IBM COBOL 85 extensions. Boxed words are both VAX and IBM COBOL 85 extensions.

ACCEPT
ACCESS
ACTUAL
ADD
ADVANCING
AFTER
ALL
ALLOWING
ALPHABET *
ALPHABETIC
ALPHABETIC-LOWER *
ALPHABETIC-UPPER *
ALPHANUMERIC *
ALPHANUMERIC-EDITED *
ALSO
ALTER
ALTERNATE
AND
ANY *
APPLY
ARE
AREA

CHARACTERS
CLASS *
CLOCK-UNITS
CLOSE
COBOL
CODE
CODE-SET
COLLATING
COLUMN
COM-REG
COMMA
COMMIT
COMMON
COMMUNICATION
COMP
COMP-1
COMP-2
COMP-3
COMP-4
COMP-5
COMP-6
COMPUTATIONAL

AREAS
ASCENDING
ASSIGN
AT
AUTHOR
AUTOTERMINATE

BASIS
BATCH
BEFORE
BEGINNING
BELL
BINARY *
BIT
BITS
BLANK
BLINKING
BLOCK
BOLD
BOOLEAN
BOTTOM
BY

CALL
CANCEL
CBL
CD
CF
CH
CHARACTER

COMPUTATIONAL-1
COMPUTATIONAL-2
COMPUTATIONAL-3
COMPUTATIONAL-4
COMPUTATIONAL-5
COMPUTATIONAL-6
COMPUTE
CONCURRENT
CONFIGURATION
CONNECT
CONSOLE
CONTAIN
CONTAINS
CONTENT *
CONTINUE *
CONTROL
CONTROLS
CONVERSION
CONVERTING *
COPY
CORE-INDEX
CORR
CORRESPONDING
COUNT
CURRENCY
CURRENT
CURRENT-DATE

DATA
DATE

DATE-COMPILED
DATE-WRITTEN
DAY
DAY-OF-WEEK *
DB
DB-ACCESS-CONTROL-KEY
DB-CONDITION
DB-CURRENT-RECORD-ID
DB-CURRENT-RECORD-NAME
DB-EXCEPTION
DBKEY
DB-KEY
DB-RECORD-NAME
DB-SET-NAME
DB-STATUS
DEBUG-SUB
DB-UWA
DE
DEBUG-CONTENTS
DEBUG-ITEM
DEBUG-LENGTH
DEBUG-LINE
DEBUG-NAME
DEBUG-NUMERIC-CONTENTS
DEBUG-SIZE
DEBUG-START
DEBUG-SUB
DEBUG-SUB-1
DEBUG-SUB-2
DEBUG-SUB-3

ECHO
EGCS
EGI
EJECT
ELSE
EMI
EMPTY
ENABLE
END
END-ACCEPT
END-ADD *
END-CALL *
END-COMMIT
END-COMPUTE *
END-CONNECT
END-DELETE *
END-DISCONNECT
END-DIVIDE *
END-ERASE
END-EVALUATE *
END-FETCH
END-FIND
END-FINISH
END-FREE
END-GET
END-IF *
ENDING
END-KEEP
END-MODIFY
END-MULTIPLY *

DEBUG-SUB-ITEM
DEBUG-SUB-N
DEBUG-SUM-NUM
DEBUGGING
DECIMAL-POINT
DECLARATIVES
DEFAULT
DELETE
DELIMITED
DELIMITER
DEPENDING
DESCENDING
DESCRIPTOR
DESTINATION
DETAIL
DICTIONARY
DISABLE
DISCONNECT
DISP
DISPLAY
DISPLAY-1
DISPLAY-6
DISPLAY-7
DISPLAY-9
DIVIDE
DIVISION
DOES
DOWN
DUPLICATE
DUPLICATES
DYNAMIC

END-OF-PAGE
END-PERFORM *
END-READ *
END-READY
END-RECEIVE *
END-RECONNECT
END-RETURN *
END-REWRITE *
END-ROLLBACK
END-SEARCH *
END-START *
END-STORE
END-STRING *
END-SUBTRACT *
END-UNSTRING *
END-WRITE *
ENTER
ENTRY
ENVIRONMENT
EOP
EQUAL
EQUALS
ERASE
ERROR
ESI
EVALUATE *
EVERY **
EXCEEDS
EXCEPTION
EXCLUSIVE
EXIT

EXOR
EXTEND
EXTERNAL *

FAILURE
FALSE *
FD
FETCH
FILE
FILE-CONTROL
FILE-LIMIT
FILE-LIMITS
FILLER
FINAL
FIND
FINISH
FIRST
FOOTING
FOR
FREE
FROM

GENERATE
GET
GIVING
GLOBAL *
GO
GOBACK
GREATER
GROUP

KEEP
KEY

LABEL
LAST
LD
LEADING
LEAVE
LEFT
LENGTH
LESS
LIMIT
LIMITS
LINAGE
LINAGE-COUNTER
LINE
LINE-COUNTER
LINES
LINKAGE
LOCALLY
LOCK
LOW-VALUE
LOW-VALUES

MATCH
MATCHES
MEMBER
MEMBERSHIP
MEMORY **
MERGE

HEADING
HIGH-VALUE
HIGH-VALUES

ID
IDENTIFICATION
IF
IN
INCLUDING
INDEX
INDEXED
INDICATE
INITIAL
INITIALIZE *
INITIATE
INPUT
INPUT-OUTPUT
INSERT
INSPECT
INSTALLATION
INTO
INVALID
I-O
I-O-CONTROL
IS

JUST
JUSTIFIED

KANJI

MESSAGE
MODE
MODIFY
MODULES **
MORE-LABELS
MOVE
MULTIPLE
MULTIPLY

NATIVE
NEGATIVE
NEXT
NO
NOMINAL
NON-NULL
NONE
NOT
NOTE
NULL
NULLS
NUMBER
NUMERIC
NUMERIC-EDITED

OBJECT-COMPUTER
OCCURS
OF
OFF
OFFSET
OMITTED

ON
ONLY
OPEN
OPTIONAL
OR
ORDER *
ORGANIZATION
OTHER *
OTHERS
OUTPUT
OVERFLOW
OWNER

PACKED-DECIMAL *
PADDING *
PAGE
PAGE-COUNTER
PARAGRAPH
PASSWORD
PERFORM
PF
PH
PIC
PICTURE
PLUS
POINTER
POSITION
POSITIVE
PRESENT
PRINTING

REFERENCE-MODIFIER
REFERENCES
REGARDLESS
RELATIVE
RELEASE
RELOAD
REMAINDER
REMOVAL
RENAMES
REPLACE *
REPLACING
REPORT
REPORTING
REPORTS
REREAD
RERUN
RESERVE
RESET
RETAINING
RETRIEVAL
RETURN
RETURN-CODE
REVERSED
REWIND
REWRITE
RF
RH
RIGHT
RMS-FILENAME
RMS-STS

PRIOR
PROCEDURE
PROCEDURES
PROCEED
PROGRAM
PROGRAM-ID
PROTECTED
PURGE *

QUEUE
QUOTE
QUOTES

RANDOM
RD
READ
READERS
READY
REALM
REALMS
RECEIVE
RECONNECT
RECORD
RECORD-NAME
RECORD-OVERFLOW
RECORDING
RECORDS
REDEFINES
REEL
REFERENCE *

RMS-STV
ROLLBACK
ROUNDED
RUN

SAME
SCREEN
SD
SEARCH
SECTION
SECURITY
SEGMENT
SEGMENT-LIMIT
SELECT
SEND
SENTENCE
SEPARATE
SEQUENCE
SEQUENCE-NUMBER
SEQUENTIAL
SERVICE
SET
SETS
SHIFT-IN
SHIFT-OUT
SIGN
SIZE
SKIP-1
SKIP-2
SKIP-3

SORT
SORT-CONTROL
SORT-CORE-SIZE
SORT-FILE-SIZE
SORT-MERGE
SORT-MESSAGE
SORT-MODE-SIZE
SORT-RETURN
SOURCE
SOURCE-COMPUTER
SPACE
SPACES
SPECIAL-NAMES
STANDARD
STANDARD-1
STANDARD-2 *
START
STATUS
STOP
STORE
STRING
SUB-QUEUE-1
SUB-QUEUE-2
SUB-QUEUE-3
SUB-SCHEMA
SUBTRACT
SUCCESS
SUM
SUPPRESS
SYMBOLIC
SYNC

TOP
TRAILING
TRUE *
TYPE

UNDERLINED
UNEQUAL
UNIT
UNLOCK
UNSTRING
UNTIL
UP
UPDATE
UPDATERS
UPON
USAGE
USAGE-MODE
USE
USING

VALUE
VALUES
VARYING

WAIT
WHEN
WHEN-COMPILED
WHERE
WITH
WITHIN
WORDS **

```
SYNCHRONIZED

TABLE
TALLY
TALLYING
TAPE
TENANT
TERMINAL
TERMINATE
TEST
TEXT
THAN
THEN *
THROUGH
THRU
TIME
TIME-OF-DAY
TIMES
TITLE
TO

WORKING-STORAGE
WRITE
WRITE-ONLY
WRITERS

ZERO
ZEROES
ZEROS

+
-
*
/
**
>
<
=
>= *
<= *
```

III. Complete COBOL Language Formats

This guide contains the composite language formats of the American National Standard COBOL. Shaded entries are those that are applicable to COBOL 85 only. Entries in blue are IBM extensions. Entries in red are VAX extensions. Entries with an * are both IBM and VAX extensions.

General Format for IDENTIFICATION DIVISION

```
{ IDENTIFICATION DIVISION. }
{ ID DIVISION.             }

PROGRAM-ID.   program-name   [ IS { | COMMON  | } PROGRAM ] .
                                  { | INITIAL | }

[AUTHOR.   [comment-entry] . . . ]
[INSTALLATION.   [comment-entry] . . . ]
[DATE-WRITTEN.   [comment-entry] . . . ]
[DATE-COMPILED.   [comment-entry] . . . ]
[SECURITY.   [comment-entry] . . . ]
```

General Format for ENVIRONMENT DIVISION*

```
[ENVIRONMENT  DIVISION.
[CONFIGURATION  SECTION.
[SOURCE-COMPUTER.   [computer-name   [WITH DEBUGGING MODE].]]
[OBJECT-COMPUTER.   [computcr-namc
    [PROGRAM COLLATING SEQUENCE IS alphabet-name-1]
    [SEGMENT-LIMIT IS segment-number].]]
```

[SPECIAL-NAMES. [[implementor-name-1

{IS mnemonic-name-1 [ON STATUS IS condition-name-1 [OFF STATUS IS condition-name-2]]
IS mnemonic-name-2 [OFF STATUS IS condition-name-2 [ON STATUS IS condition-name-1]]
ON STATUS IS condition-name-1 [OFF STATUS IS condition-name-2]
OFF STATUS IS condition-name-2 [ON STATUS IS condition-name-1]}] . . .

[ALPHABET alphabet-name-1 IS

{ASCII
EBCDIC/}

{STANDARD-1
STANDARD-2
NATIVE
implementor-name-2
{literal-1 [{THROUGH
THRU} literal-2
{ALSO literal-3} . . .]} . . .}] . . .

[SYMBOLIC CHARACTERS {{symbolic-character-1} . . . {IS
ARE} {integer-1} . . . } . . .

*The ENVIRONMENT DIVISION, CONFIGURATION SECTION, and INPUT-OUTPUT SECTION entries are required for COBOL 74.

```
        [IN alphabet-name-2]}] ...

[CLASS class-name IS  {literal-4  [{THROUGH}  literal-5]}... ] ...
                                  [{THRU   }
[CURRENCY SIGN IS literal-6]
[DECIMAL-POINT IS COMMA].]]]
[INPUT-OUTPUT SECTION.
FILE-CONTROL.
    {file-control-entry} ...
[I-O-CONTROL.
    [[      [RECORD    ]                                        ]
    [[ SAME [SORT      ] AREA FOR file-name-1 {file-name-2} ... ] ...
    [[      [SORT-MERGE]                                        ]
    [MULTIPLE FILE TAPE CONTAINS
        {file-name-3 [POSITION integer-1] } ... ] ... .]]]]
```

General Format for FILE-CONTROL Entry

SEQUENTIAL FILE

```
SELECT [OPTIONAL] file-name-1
```

ASSIGN TO {implementor-name-1 | literal-1} . . .

[RESERVE integer-1 [AREA | AREAS]]

[[ORGANIZATION IS] SEQUENTIAL]

[BLOCK CONTAINS [smallest-block TO] blocksize {RECORDS | CHARACTERS}]

[CODE-SET IS alpha-name]

[PADDING CHARACTER IS {data-name-1 | literal-2}]

[RECORD DELIMITER IS {STANDARD-1 | implementor-name-2}]

[ACCESS MODE IS SEQUENTIAL]
[FILE STATUS IS data-name-2].

RELATIVE FILE

SELECT [OPTIONAL] file-name-1

ASSIGN TO {implementor-name-1 | literal-1} . . .

[RESERVE integer-1 [AREA | AREAS]]

```
[ORGANIZATION IS] RELATIVE

[BLOCK CONTAINS [smallest-block TO] blocksize {RECORDS   }]
                                              {CHARACTERS}

[PASSWORD IS data-name]

[ACCESS MODE IS {SEQUENTIAL [RELATIVE KEY IS data-name-1]  }]
[               {{RANDOM }                                 }]
[               {{DYNAMIC} RELATIVE KEY IS data-name-1     }]

[FILE STATUS IS data-name-2].
```

INDEXED FILE

```
SELECT [OPTIONAL] file-name-1

    ASSIGN TO {implementor-name-1} ...
              {literal-1         }

    [RESERVE integer-1 [AREA ]]
                       [AREAS]

    [ORGANIZATION IS] INDEXED

    [BLOCK CONTAINS [smallest-block TO] blocksize {RECORDS   }]
                                                  {CHARACTERS}

    [PASSWORD IS data-name]
```

```
[ACCESS MODE IS {SEQUENTIAL | RANDOM | DYNAMIC}]

RECORD KEY IS data-name-1
[ALTERNATE RECORD KEY IS data-name-2 [WITH DUPLICATES]] . . .
[FILE STATUS IS data-name-3].
```

SORT OR MERGE FILE

```
SELECT file-name-1   ASSIGN TO {implementor-name-1 | literal-1} . . .  .
```

REPORT FILE

```
SELECT [OPTIONAL] file-name-1
    ASSIGN TO {implementor-name-1 | literal-1} . . .
    [RESERVE integer-1 [AREA | AREAS]]
    [[ORGANIZATION IS] SEQUENTIAL]
    [BLOCK CONTAINS [smallest-block TO] blocksize {RECORDS | CHARACTERS}]
    [CODE-SET IS alpha-name]
```

```
[PADDING CHARACTER IS {data-name-1 | literal-1}]
[RECORD DELIMITER IS {STANDARD-1 | implementor-name-2}]
[ACCESS MODE IS SEQUENTIAL]
[FILE STATUS IS data-name-2].
```

General Format—I-O-CONTROL

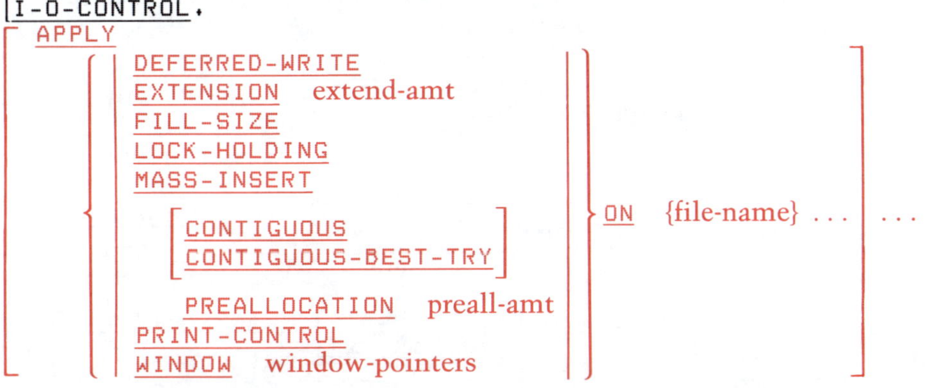

```
[I-O-CONTROL.
[ APPLY
     { DEFERRED-WRITE
       EXTENSION extend-amt
       FILL-SIZE
       LOCK-HOLDING
       MASS-INSERT
         [CONTIGUOUS
          CONTIGUOUS-BEST-TRY]
         PREALLOCATION preall-amt
       PRINT-CONTROL
       WINDOW window-pointers } ON {file-name} . . . ] . . .
```

```
[ ; RERUN [ ON {file-name-1          } ]
                {implementor-name     }

              {   { [END OF] {REEL}  }                   }
              {   {          {UNIT}  }  OF  file-name-2  }
        EVERY {   { integer-1 RECORDS}                   }  ] ...
              { integer-2  CLOCK-UNITS                   }
              { condition-name                           }

[ ; SAME [RECORD    ] AREA FOR  file-name-3  {, file-name-4} ... ] ...
         [SORT      ]
         [SORT-MERGE]

[; MULTIPLE FILE TAPE CONTAINS  file-name-5  [POSITION  integer-3]

      [, file-name-6  [POSITION  integer-4]] ... ] ... ]].
```

General Format for DATA DIVISION

```
[DATA DIVISION.
[SUB-SCHEMA SECTION.   [subschema-entry   [keeplist-entry] ... ]]
[FILE SECTION.
[file-description-entry
{record-description-entry} ... ] ...
[sort-merge-file-description-entry
{record-description-entry} ... ] ...
[report-file-description-entry] ... ]
```

```
[WORKING-STORAGE SECTION.
[77-level-description-entry ] ... ]
[record-description-entry   ]
[LINKAGE SECTION.
[77-level-description-entry ] ... ]
[record-description-entry   ]
[COMMUNICATION SECTION.
[communication-description-entry
[record-description-entry] ... ] ... ]
[REPORT SECTION.
[report-description-entry
{report-group-description-entry} ... ] ... ]]
```

General Format—Subschema Description

```
DB  subschema-name  WITHIN  schema-name
    [FOR  database-name]  [{THRU   }  stream-name]
                           {THROUGH}
```

General Format—Keeplist Description

```
LD  keeplist-name  [LIMIT IS  integer].
```

General Format for File Description Entry

SEQUENTIAL FILE

```
FD  file-name-1
    [IS EXTERNAL]
    [IS GLOBAL]
    [BLOCK CONTAINS [integer-1 TO] integer-2 {RECORDS   }]
                                             {CHARACTERS}]

    [        {CONTAINS integer-3 CHARACTERS                                          }]
    [RECORD  {IS VARYING IN SIZE [[FROM integer-4] [TO integer-5] CHARACTERS]         }]
    [        {        [DEPENDING ON data-name-1]                                     }]
    [        {CONTAINS integer-6 TO integer-7 CHARACTERS                             }]

    [LABEL {RECORD IS   } {STANDARD}]
    [      {RECORDS ARE } {OMITTED }]

    [VALUE OF {implementor-name-1 IS {data-name-2}} . . .]
    [                                {literal-1  }      ]

    [DATA {RECORD IS  } {data-name-3} . . .]
    [     {RECORDS ARE}                    ]

    [LINAGE IS {data-name-4} LINES [WITH FOOTING AT {data-name-5}]
    [          {integer-8  }       [                {integer-9  }]

          [LINES AT TOP {data-name-6}] [LINES AT BOTTOM {data-name-7}]]
          [             {integer-10 }] [                {integer-11 }]]
```

```
[CODE-SET IS alphabet-name-1].
[[ACCESS MODE IS] SEQUENTIAL]
[FILE STATUS IS file-status].
```

RELATIVE FILE

```
FD  file-name-1
    [IS EXTERNAL]
    [IS GLOBAL]
    [BLOCK CONTAINS [integer-1 TO] integer-2 {RECORDS    }]
                                             {CHARACTERS }
    [         {CONTAINS integer-3 CHARACTERS                                          }]
    [RECORD   {IS VARYING IN SIZE [[FROM integer-4] [TO integer-5] CHARACTERS]        }]
    [         {        [DEPENDING ON data-name-1]                                     }]
    [         {CONTAINS integer-6 TO integer-7 CHARACTERS                             }]
    [LABEL {RECORD IS  } {STANDARD}]
    [      {RECORDS ARE} {OMITTED }]
    [VALUE OF {implementor-name-1 IS {data-name-2}} ... ]
    [                                {literal-1  }      ]
    [DATA {RECORD IS  } {data-name-3} ... ].
    [     {RECORDS ARE}                    ]
    [[ACCESS MODE IS] {SEQUENTIAL [RELATIVE KEY IS rel-key]        }]
    [                 {  {RANDOM } RELATIVE KEY IS rel-key         }]
    [                 {  {DYNAMIC}                                 }]
```

[FILE STATUS IS file-status]

INDEXED FILE

```
FD  file-name-1
    [IS EXTERNAL]
    [IS GLOBAL]
    [BLOCK CONTAINS [integer-1 TO] integer-2 {RECORDS    }]
                                             {CHARACTERS }
    [RECORD {CONTAINS integer-3 CHARACTERS                                          }]
            {IS VARYING IN SIZE [[FROM integer-4] [TO integer-5] CHARACTERS]        }
            {        [DEPENDING ON data-name-1]                                     }
            {CONTAINS integer-6 TO integer-7 CHARACTERS                             }
    [LABEL {RECORD IS   } {STANDARD}]
           {RECORDS ARE } {OMITTED }
    [VALUE OF {implementor-name-1 IS {data-name-2}} ...]
                                     {literal-1  }
    [DATA {RECORD IS   } (data-name-3) ...].
          {RECORDS ARE }
    [[ACCESS MODE IS] {SEQUENTIAL}]
                      {RANDOM    }
                      {DYNAMIC   }
    RECORD KEY IS rec-key
    [ALTERNATE RECORD KEY IS alt-key [WITH DUPLICATES]] ...
    [FILE STATUS IS file-status].
```

SORT-MERGE FILE

```
SD  file-name-1
    [ RECORD  { CONTAINS integer-1 CHARACTERS                                          } ]
    [         { IS VARYING IN SIZE [[FROM integer-2] [TO integer-3] CHARACTERS]        } ]
    [         {       [DEPENDING ON data-name-1]                                       } ]
    [         { CONTAINS integer-4 TO integer-5 CHARACTERS                             } ]

    [ DATA  { RECORD IS   }  {data-name-2} . . . ]
    [       { RECORDS ARE }                      ]
```

REPORT FILE

```
FD  file-name-1
    [IS EXTERNAL]
    [IS GLOBAL]
    [ BLOCK CONTAINS  [integer-1 TO]  integer-2  { RECORDS    } ]
    [                                            { CHARACTERS } ]

    [ RECORD  { CONTAINS integer-3 CHARACTERS                                          } ]
    [         { IS VARYING IN SIZE [[FROM integer-4] [TO integer-5] CHARACTERS]        } ]
    [         {       [DEPENDING ON data-name-1]                                       } ]
    [         { CONTAINS integer-6 TO integer-7 CHARACTERS                             } ]

    [ LABEL  { RECORD IS   }  { STANDARD } ]
    [        { RECORDS ARE }  { OMITTED  } ]

    [ VALUE OF  { implementor-name-1 IS  { data-name-2 } } . . . ]
    [           {                        { literal-1   } }       ]
```

[[ACCESS MODE IS] SEQUENTIAL]
[CODE-SET IS alphabet-name-1]
{REPORT IS / REPORTS ARE} {report-name-1} . . .
[FILE STATUS IS file-status].

General Format for Data Description Entry

FORMAT 1

level-number [data-name-1 / FILLER]

[REDEFINES data-name-2]
[IS EXTERNAL]
[IS GLOBAL]
[{PICTURE / PIC} IS character-string]

```
[USAGE IS] { BINARY
             COMPUTATIONAL-1*
             COMP-1*
             COMPUTATIONAL-2*
             COMP-2*
             COMPUTATIONAL-3*
             COMP-3*
             DISPLAY
             DISPLAY-1*
             INDEX
             PACKED-DECIMAL
             POINTER* }

[[SIGN IS] { LEADING
             TRAILING }  [SEPARATE CHARACTER]]

[ OCCURS integer-2 TIMES
      [{ ASCENDING
         DESCENDING }  KEY IS  {data-name-3} . . . ] . . .
      [INDEXED BY  {index-name-1} . . . ]
  OCCURS integer-1 TO integer-2 TIMES DEPENDING ON data-name-4
      [{ ASCENDING
         DESCENDING }  KEY IS  {data-name-3} . . . ] . . .
      [INDEXED BY  {index-name-1} . . . ] ]
```

```
[ { SYNCHRONIZED }  [ LEFT  ] ]
[ { SYNC         }  [ RIGHT ] ]

[ { JUSTIFIED }  RIGHT ]
[ { JUST      }        ]

[                 { ZERO   } ]
[ BLANK WHEN      { ZEROES } ]
[                 { ZEROS  } ]

[            { literal-1                    } ]
[            { EXTERNAL   external-name     } ]
[ VALUE IS   { REFERENCE  data-name         } ].
[            { NULL                         } ]
[            { NULLS                        } ]
```

FORMAT 2

```
66   data-name-1 RENAMES data-name-2   [ { THROUGH }   data-name-3 ].
                                       [ { THRU    }               ]
```

FORMAT 3

```
                        { literal-1                          }
                        { EXTERNAL   external-name           }
                        { REFERENCE  data-name               }
88 condition-name-1     { low-val                            }
   { VALUE IS   }                                              ...
   { VALUES ARE }       [ { THROUGH }  { literal-2                  } ]
                        [ { THRU    }  { EXTERNAL   external-name   } ]
                        [              { REFERENCE  data-name       } ]
                        [              { high-val                   } ]
```

FORMAT 1

```
CD  cd-name-1

                                [[SYMBOLIC QUEUE IS data-name-1]
                                    [SYMBOLIC SUB-QUEUE-1 IS data-name-2]
                                    [SYMBOLIC SUB-QUEUE-2 IS data-name-3]
                                    [SYMBOLIC SUB-QUEUE-3 IS data-name-4]
                                    [MESSAGE DATE IS data-name-5]
                                    [MESSAGE TIME IS data-name-6]
                                    [SYMBOLIC SOURCE IS data-name-7]
    FOR  [INITIAL]  INPUT           [TEXT LENGTH IS data-name-8]
                                    [END KEY IS data-name-9]
                                    [STATUS KEY IS data-name-10]
                                    [MESSAGE COUNT IS data-name-11]]
                                [data-name-1, data-name-2, data-name-3,
                                    data-name-4, data-name-5, data-name-6,
                                    data-name-7, data-name-8, data-name-9,
                                    data-name-10, data-name-11]
```

FORMAT 2

```
CD  cd-name-1 FOR OUTPUT
    [DESTINATION COUNT IS data-name-1]
    [TEXT LENGTH IS data-name-2]
    [STATUS KEY IS data-name-3]
    [DESTINATION TABLE OCCURS integer-1 TIMES
        [INDEXED BY {index-name-1} . . . ]]
    [ERROR KEY IS data-name-4]
    [SYMBOLIC DESTINATION IS data-name-5].
```

FORMAT 3

```
CD  cd-name-1
                        ┌ [[MESSAGE DATE IS data-name-1]          ┐
                        │      [MESSAGE TIME IS data-name-2]      │
                        │      [SYMBOLIC TERMINAL IS data-name-3] │
    FOR [INITIAL] I-O   │      [TEXT LENGTH IS data-name-4]       │
                        │      [END KEY IS data-name-5]           │
                        │      [STATUS KEY IS data-name-6]]       │
                        │ [data-name-1, data-name-2, data-name-3, │
                        └      data-name-4, data-name-5, data-name-6] ┘
```

General Format for Report Description Entry

```
RD  report-name-1
    [IS GLOBAL]
    [CODE literal-1]
```

```
[{CONTROL IS  } {{data-name-1} . . .          }]
[{CONTROLS ARE} {FINAL [data-name-1] . . .    }]

[PAGE [LIMIT IS  ] integer-1 [LINE ] [HEADING integer-2]
[     [LIMITS ARE]           [LINES]

      [FIRST DETAIL integer-3] [LAST DETAIL integer-4]

      [FOOTING integer-5]].
```

General Format for Report Group Description Entry

FORMAT 1

```
01   [data-name-1]

     [LINE NUMBER IS  {integer-1  [ON NEXT PAGE]}]
     [                {PLUS integer-2           }]

     [                {integer-3     }]
     [NEXT GROUP IS   {PLUS integer-4}]
     [                {NEXT PAGE     }]
```

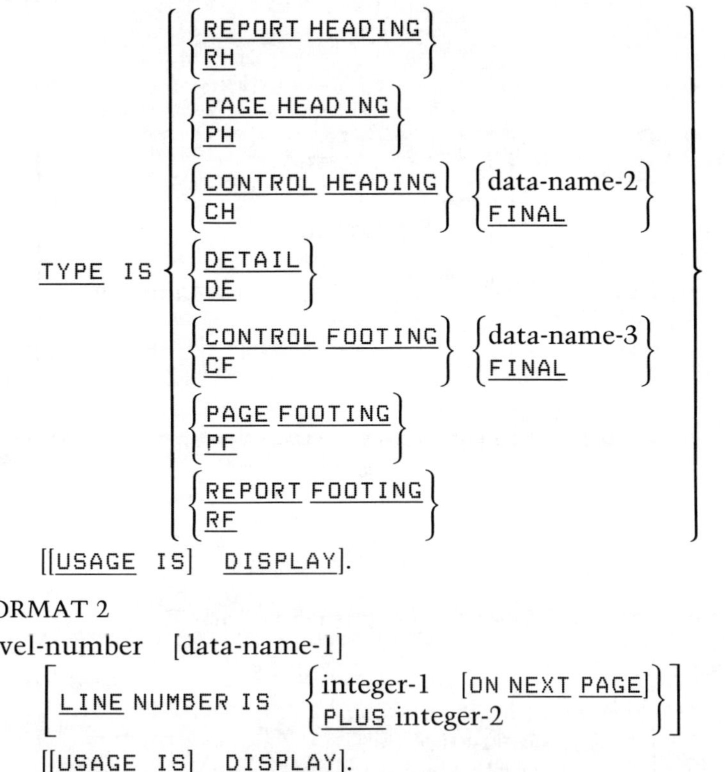

```
TYPE IS { {REPORT HEADING | RH}
          {PAGE HEADING | PH}
          {CONTROL HEADING | CH} {data-name-2 | FINAL}
          {DETAIL | DE}
          {CONTROL FOOTING | CF} {data-name-3 | FINAL}
          {PAGE FOOTING | PF}
          {REPORT FOOTING | RF} }
[[USAGE IS] DISPLAY].
```

FORMAT 2

```
level-number [data-name-1]
   [LINE NUMBER IS {integer-1 [ON NEXT PAGE] | PLUS integer-2}]
   [[USAGE IS] DISPLAY].
```

FORMAT 3

```
level-number   [data-name-1]

        {PICTURE}  IS character-string
        {PIC    }

        [[USAGE IS] DISPLAY]

        [ [SIGN IS] {LEADING } SEPARATE CHARACTER ]
        [           {TRAILING}                    ]

        [ {JUSTIFIED}  RIGHT ]
        [ {JUST     }        ]

        [BLANK WHEN ZERO]

        [ LINE NUMBER IS  {integer-1  [ON NEXT PAGE]} ]
        [                 {PLUS integer-2           } ]

        [COLUMN NUMBER IS integer-3]

        { SOURCE IS identifier-1                                          }
        { VALUE IS literal-1                                              }
        { {SUM {identifier-2} ...  [UPON {data-name-2} ... ] } ...        }
        {        [ RESET ON  {data-name-3} ]                              }
        {        [           {FINAL      } ]                              }

        [GROUP INDICATE].
```

General Format for PROCEDURE DIVISION

FORMAT 1

```
[PROCEDURE DIVISION  [USING  {data-name-1} ... ]  [GIVING  identifier-1].
[DECLARATIVES.
{section-name SECTION [segment-number].
     USE statement.
[paragraph-name.
     [sentence] ... ] ... } ...
 END DECLARATIVES.]
{section-name SECTION [segment-number].
[paragraph-name.
     [sentence] ... ] ... } ... ]
```

FORMAT 2

```
[PROCEDURE DIVISION  [USING  {data-name-1} ... ]  [GIVING  identifier-1].
{paragraph-name.
     [sentence] ... } ... ]
```

General Format for COBOL Verbs

```
ACCEPT identifier-1   [FROM  mnemonic-name-1]
     [AT END   imperative statement-1]
     [NOT AT END   imperative statement-2]
     [END-ACCEPT]
```

```
ACCEPT identifier-2 FROM { DATE        }
                         { DAY         }
                         { DAY-OF-WEEK }
                         { TIME        }

ACCEPT   dest-item
{ |                             { line-num                             } | }
{ |   FROM LINE NUMBER          { line-id    [PLUS    [plus-num]]      } | }
{ |                             { PLUS    [plus-num]                   } | }
{ |                                                                      | }
{ |                             { column-num                           } | }
{ |   FROM COLUMN NUMBER        { column-id    [PLUS    [plus-num]]    } | }
{ |                             { PLUS    [plus-num]                   } | }
{ |                                                                      | }
{ |   ERASE   [TO END OF]       { SCREEN }                               | }
{ |                             { LINE   }                               | }
{ |   WITH BELL                                                          | }
{ |   UNDERLINED                                                         | }
{ |   BOLD                                                               | }
{ |   WITH BLINKING                                                      | }
{ |                                                                      | }
{ |              [ { | SIZE { prot-size-lit  }               | } ]       | }
{ |              [ { |      { prot-size-item }               | } ]       | }
{ |   PROTECTED  [ { |                                       | } ]       | }
{ |              [ { | WITH AUTOTERMINATE                    | } ]       | }
{ |              [ { | WITH NO BLANK                         | } ]       | }
{ |              [ { | WITH FILLER prot-fill-lit             | } ]       | }
```

```
      WITH CONVERSION
      REVERSED
      WITH NO ECHO
                   { def-src-lit       }
      DEFAULT IS   { def-src-item      }
                   { CURRENT VALUE     }
      CONTROL KEY IN key-dest-item

  [ { [ON EXCEPTION stment] [NOT ON EXCEPTION stment2] } ]
  [ { [AT END stment] [NOT AT END stment2]             } ]

  [END-ACCEPT]
ACCEPT  CONTROL KEY IN key-dest-item
                         { line-num                     }
      FROM LINE NUMBER   { line-id  [PLUS  [plus-num]]  }
                         { PLUS  [plus-num]             }

                         { column-num                    }
      FROM COLUMN NUMBER { column-id  [PLUS  [plus-num]] }
                         { PLUS  [plus-num]              }

      ERASE  [TO END OF]  { SCREEN }
                          { LINE   }
      WITH BELL

  [ { [ON EXCEPTION stment] [NOT ON EXCEPTION stment2] } ]
  [ { [AT END stment] [NOT AT END stment2]             } ]
```

```
    [END-ACCEPT]
ACCEPT cd-name-1 MESSAGE COUNT

ADD {identifier-1} ... TO {identifier-2 [ROUNDED]} ...
    {literal-1   }

   [ON SIZE ERROR imperative-statement-1]
   [NOT ON SIZE ERROR imperative-statement-2]
   [END-ADD]

ADD {identifier-1} ... TO {identifier-2}
    {literal-1   }        {literal-2   }

    GIVING {identifier-3 [ROUNDED]} ...
    [ON SIZE ERROR imperative-statement-1]
    [NOT ON SIZE ERROR imperative-statement-2]
    [END-ADD]

ADD {CORRESPONDING} identifier-1 TO identifier-2 [ROUNDED]
    {CORR         }

    [ON SIZE ERROR imperative-statement-1]
    [NOT ON SIZE ERROR imperative-statement-2]
    [END-ADD]

ALTER {procedure-name-1 TO [PROCEED TO] procedure-name-2} ...

CALL {identifier-1} [USING {[BY REFERENCE] {identifier-2} ...} ... ]
     {literal-1   }        {BY CONTENT {identifier-2} ...     }
```

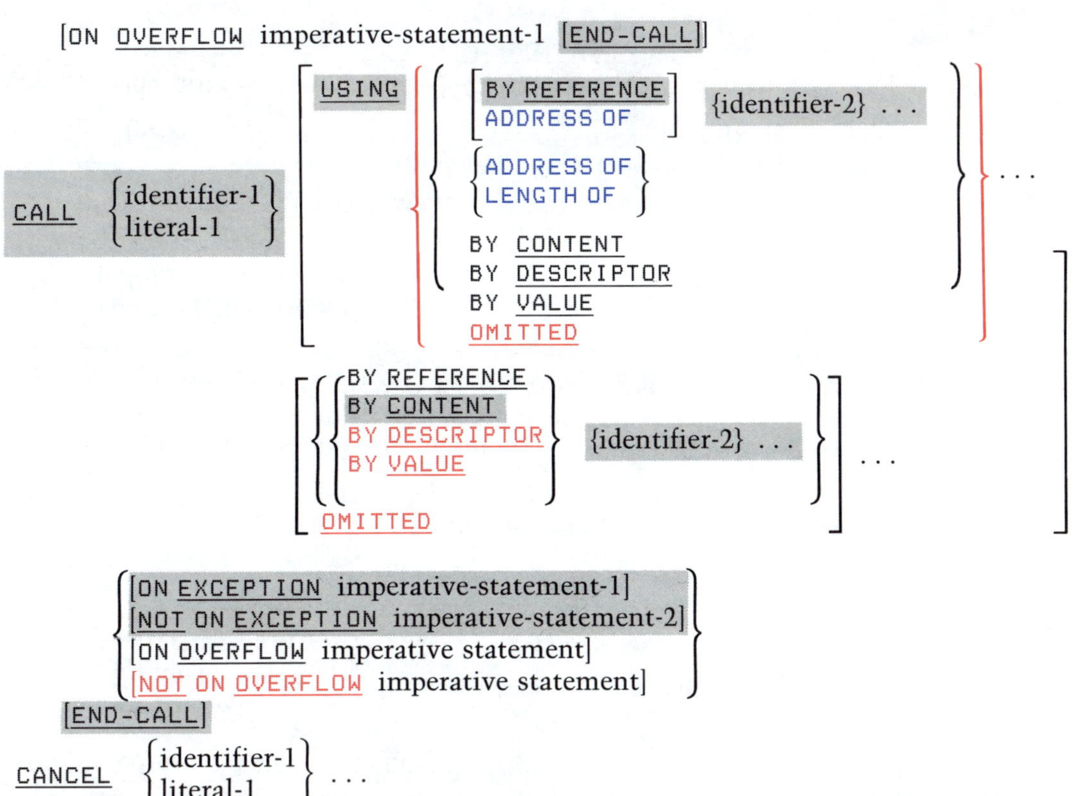

```
[ON OVERFLOW imperative-statement-1 [END-CALL]]

CALL {identifier-1}
     {literal-1   }
  [USING { { [BY REFERENCE] {identifier-2} . . . } } . . . ]
         { { [ADDRESS OF  ]                      } }
         { { {ADDRESS OF}                        } }
         { { {LENGTH OF }                        } }
         { { BY CONTENT                          } }
         { { BY DESCRIPTOR                       } }
         {   BY VALUE                              }
         {   OMITTED                               }
  [ [ { {BY REFERENCE } {identifier-2} . . . } ] . . . ]
  [ [ { {BY CONTENT   }                      } ]       ]
  [ [ { {BY DESCRIPTOR}                      } ]       ]
  [ [ { {BY VALUE     }                      } ]       ]
  [ [ OMITTED                                  ]       ]
  {[ON EXCEPTION imperative-statement-1]    }
  {[NOT ON EXCEPTION imperative-statement-2]}
  {[ON OVERFLOW imperative statement]       }
  {[NOT ON OVERFLOW imperative statement]   }
  [END-CALL]

CANCEL {identifier-1} . . .
       {literal-1   }
```

```
                         ┌ ┌REEL┐                          ┐ ┐
                         │ │UNIT│   [FOR REMOVAL]          │ │
SW CLOSE   { file-name-1 │                                 │ } ...
                         │ WITH  ┌NO REWIND┐               │ │
                         └       └LOCK     ┘               ┘ ┘

RI CLOSE   {file-name-1  [WITH LOCK]} ...
```

```
COMMIT [RETAINING]
    [ON ERROR stment]
    [NOT ON ERROR stment2]
    [END-COMMIT]
```

```
                                          { =     }
COMPUTE  {identifier-1 [ROUNDED]} ...     { EQUAL } arithmetic-expression-1

    [ON SIZE ERROR imperative-statement-1]
    [NOT ON SIZE ERROR imperative-statement-2]
    [END-COMPUTE]
```

```
                              { {set-name} ... }
CONNECT [record-name] TO      { ALL            }

    [ RETAINING [ { | REALM                      | } ] CURRENCY ]
    [           [ { | RECORD                     | } ]          ]
    [           [ { | { SET [set-name] ...  }    | } ]          ]
    [           [ { | { {set-name} ...      }    | } ]          ]

    [ON ERROR stment] [NOT ON ERROR stment2]
    [END-CONNECT]
```

```
CONTINUE
DELETE file-name-1 RECORD
    [INVALID KEY imperative-statement-1]
    [NOT INVALID KEY imperative-statement-2]
    [END-DELETE]

        { INPUT [TERMINAL] }
DISABLE { I-O TERMINAL     } cd-name-1
        { OUTPUT           }

DISCONNECT [record-name] FROM { {set-name} ... }
                              { ALL            }
    [ON ERROR stment]
    [NOT ON ERROR stment2]
    [END-DISCONNECT]

                                  { CONSOLE           }
DISPLAY { identifier-1 } ... [UPON { SYSOUT            } [WITH NO ADVANCING]
        { literal-1    }          { mnemonic-name-1]  }
```

```
DISPLAY {src-item
   [ { | AT LINE NUMBER
       |        { line-num                         }
       |        { line-id   [PLUS   [plus-num]]    }
       |        { PLUS   [plus-num]                }
       | AT COLUMN NUMBER
       |        { column-num                       }
       |        { column-id   [PLUS   [plus-num]]  }
       |        { PLUS   [plus-num]                }
       | ERASE  [TO END OF]  { SCREEN }
       |                     { LINE   }
       | WITH BELL
       | UNDERLINED
       | BOLD
       | WITH BLINKING
       | REVERSED
       | WITH CONVERSION                              | } ] } . . .
        [WITH NO ADVANCING]
```

```
DIVIDE {identifier-1} INTO {identifier-2} GIVING identifier-3 [ROUNDED]
       {literal-1   }      {literal-2   }
    REMAINDER identifier-4
    [ON SIZE ERROR imperative-statement-1]
```

```
    [NOT ON SIZE ERROR imperative-statement-2]
    [END-DIVIDE]

DIVIDE {identifier-1}  BY  {identifier-2}  GIVING identifier-3 [ROUNDED]
       {literal-1   }      {literal-2   }
    REMAINDER identifier-4
    [ON SIZE ERROR imperative-statement-1]
    [NOT ON SIZE ERROR imperative-statement-2]
    [END-DIVIDE]

DIVIDE {identifier-1}  INTO  {identifier-2 [ROUNDED]} . . .
       {literal-1   }
    [ON SIZE ERROR imperative-statement-1]
    [NOT ON SIZE ERROR imperative-statement-2]
    [END-DIVIDE]

DIVIDE {identifier-1}  INTO  {identifier-2}
       {literal-1   }        {literal-2   }
    GIVING {identifier-3 [ROUNDED]} . . .
    [ON SIZE ERROR imperative-statement-1]
    [NOT ON SIZE ERROR imperative-statement-2]
    [END-DIVIDE]

DIVIDE {identifier-1}  BY  {identifier-2}
       {literal-1   }      {literal-2   }
    GIVING {identifier-3 [ROUNDED]} . . .
    [ON SIZE ERROR imperative-statement-1]
```

```
[NOT ON SIZE ERROR imperative-statement-2]
[END-DIVIDE]
```

```
        { INPUT [TERMINAL] }
ENABLE  { I-O TERMINAL     }  cd-name-1
        { OUTPUT           }
```

```
ENTRY literal USING identifier-1 ...
ERASE [ALL] [record-name]
      [ON ERROR stment]
      [NOT ON ERROR stment2]
      [END-ERASE]
```

```
          { identifier-1 }  [      { identifier-2 } ]
          { literal-1    }  [      { literal-2    } ]
EVALUATE  { expression-1 }  [ ALSO { expression-2 } ] ...
          { TRUE         }  [      { TRUE         } ]
          { FALSE        }  [      { FALSE        } ]
```

```
   {{WHEN

  { ANY                                                                                              }
  { condition-1                                                                                      }
  { TRUE                                                                                             }
  { FALSE                                                                                            }
  {        {{ identifier-3              }  [ { THROUGH }  { identifier-4              } ]}          }
  { [NOT]  {{ literal-3                 }  [ { THRU    }  { literal-4                 } ]}          }
  {        {{ arithmetic-expression-1   }  [              { arithmetic-expression-2   } ]}          }
```

```
[ALSO
  { ANY
    condition-2
    TRUE
    FALSE
    [NOT] {{identifier-5 | literal-5 | arithmetic-expression-3}
          [{THROUGH | THRU} {identifier-6 | literal-6 | arithmetic-expression-4}]} } ] . . . } . . .
 imperative-statement-1} . . .
[WHEN OTHER imperative-statement-2]
[END-EVALUATE]
EXIT
EXIT PROGRAM
FETCH database-record
    [FOR UPDATE]
    [RETAINING [{ | REALM
                  | RECORD
                  | {SET [set-name] . . .
                  |  {set-name} . . .     } | }] CURRENCY ]
    [{[AT END stment] [NOT AT END stment2]
      [ON ERROR stment] [NOT ON ERROR stment2]}]
    [END-FETCH]
```

```
FIND database-record [FOR UPDATE]
    [ RETAINING [ { | REALM                  | } ] CURRENCY ]
    [           [ { | RECORD                 | } ]          ]
    [           [ { | {SET [set-name] . . .} | } ]          ]
    [           [ { | {{set-name} . . .    } | } ]          ]
    [ { [AT END stment] [NOT AT END stment2]       } ]
    [ { [ON ERROR stment] [NOT ON ERROR stment2]   } ]
    [END-FIND]

FIND ALL keeplist-name [record-name] [ WITHIN { realm-name } ]
                                     [        { set-name   } ]
    [ USING {rec-key} . . .  ] [FOR UPDATE]
    [ WHERE {bool-expres}    ]
    [ { [AT END stment] [NOT AT END stment2]       } ]
    [ { [ON ERROR stment] [NOT ON ERROR stment2]   } ]
    [END-FIND]

     { database-key-id                                  }
FREE {                                                  }
     { ALL [ { FROM {keeplist-name} . . . } ]           }
     {     [ { CURRENT                    } ]           }
    [ON ERROR stment]
    [NOT ON ERROR stment2]
    [END-FREE]
```

```
CENERATE  {data-name-1  }
          {report-name-1}

GET  [ record-name         ]
     [ {record-item} . . . ]
     [ON ERROR stment]
     [NOT ON ERROR stment2]
     [END-GET]

[GOBACK]

GO TO  [procedure-name-1]
GO TO  {procedure-name-1} . . .  DEPENDING ON identifier-1

IF condition-1 THEN {{statement-1} . . .} {ELSE {statement-2} . . . [END-IF]}
                    {NEXT SENTENCE      } {ELSE NEXT SENTENCE                }
                                          {END-IF                            }

INITIALIZE  {identifier-1} . . .
[            {{ALPHABETIC            }                              }      ]
[            {{ALPHANUMERIC          }                              }      ]
[            {{NUMERIC               }                              }      ]
[ REPLACING  {{ALPHANUMERIC-EDITED   } DATA BY {identifier-2}       } . . .]
[            {{NUMERIC-EDITED        }         {literal-1   }       }      ]
[            {{BBCS                  }                              }      ]
[            {{EGCS                  }                              }      ]
```

```
INITIATE {report-name-1} . . .
INSPECT identifier-1 TALLYING

{ identifier-2 FOR { CHARACTERS [ {BEFORE} INITIAL {identifier-4} ] . . .
                                  {AFTER }         {literal-2   }
                     {ALL    } { {identifier-3} [ {BEFORE} INITIAL {identifier-4} ] . . . } . . . } . . . } . . .
                     {LEADING} { {literal-1   }   {AFTER }         {literal-2   }

INSPECT identifier-1 REPLACING

{ CHARACTERS BY {identifier-5} [ {BEFORE} INITIAL {identifier-4} ] . . .
                {literal-3   }   {AFTER }         {literal-2   }
  {ALL    } { {identifier-3} BY {identifier-5} [ {BEFORE} INITIAL {identifier-4} ] . . . } . . . } . . .
  {LEADING} { {literal-1   }    {literal-3   }   {AFTER }         {literal-2   }
  {FIRST  }

INSPECT identifier-1 TALLYING

{ identifier-2 FOR { CHARACTERS [ {BEFORE} INITIAL {identifier-4} ] . . .
                                  {AFTER }         {literal-2   }
                     {ALL    } { {identifier-3} [ {BEFORE} INITIAL {identifier-4} ] . . . } . . . } . . . } . . .
                     {LEADING} { {literal-1   }   {AFTER }         {literal-2   }
```

```
REPLACING
  { CHARACTERS BY {identifier-5} [{BEFORE} INITIAL {identifier-4}] ...
                  {literal-3   } [{AFTER }         {literal-2   }]
    {ALL    } {{identifier-3} BY {identifier-5} [{BEFORE} INITIAL {identifier-4}] ...} ... } ...
    {LEADING} {{literal-1   }    {literal-3   } [{AFTER }         {literal-2   }]    }
    {FIRST  }

INSPECT identifier-1 CONVERTING {identifier-6} TO {identifier-7}
                                {literal-4   }    {literal-5   }
    [{BEFORE} INITIAL {identifier-4}] ...
    [{AFTER }         {literal-2   }]

KEEP [database-key-id] USING destination-keeplist
    [ON ERROR imperative statement-1]
    [NOT ON ERROR imperative statement-2]
    [END-KEEP]

MERGE file-name-1 {ON {ASCENDING } KEY {data-name-1} ...} ...
                  {   {DESCENDING}                      }
    [COLLATING SEQUENCE IS alphabet-name-1]
    USING file-name-2 {file-name-3} ...
    { OUTPUT PROCEDURE IS procedure-name-1 [{THROUGH} procedure-name-2] }
    {                                      [{THRU   }                 ] }
    { GIVING {file-name-4} ...                                          }
```

```
MODIFY [ record-name          ]
       [ {record-item} . . .  ]

    [ RETAINING [ { |  REALM                                | } ] CURRENCY ]
    [           [ { |  RECORD                               | } ]          ]
    [           [ { | { SET [set-name] . . . }              | } ]          ]
    [           [ { | { {set-name} . . .     }              | } ]          ]

[ON ERROR stment]
[NOT ON ERROR stment2]
[END-MODIFY]

MOVE { identifier-1 }  TO  {identifier-2} . . .
     { literal-1    }

MOVE { CORRESPONDING }  identifier-1 TO identifier-2
     { CORR          }

MULTIPLY { identifier-1 } BY {identifier-2 [ROUNDED]} . . .
         { literal-1    }

    [ON SIZE ERROR imperative-statement-1]
    [NOT ON SIZE ERROR imperative-statement-2]
    [END-MULTIPLY]

MULTIPLY { identifier-1 } BY { identifier-2 }
         { literal-1    }    { literal-2    }
```

```
GIVING {identifier-3 [ROUNDED]} . . .
[ON SIZE ERROR imperative-statement-1]
[NOT ON SIZE ERROR imperative-statement-2]
[END-MULTIPLY]

S OPEN  { INPUT {file-name-1   [WITH NO REWIND]} . . .
        { OUTPUT {file-name-2   [WITH NO REWIND]} . . .  } . . .
        { [ALLOWING
        {    { NO OTHERS
        {    { READERS
        {    { WRITERS
        {    { UPDATERS
        {    { ALL        ]
        { I-O {file-name-3} . . .
        { EXTEND {file-name-4} . . .

RI OPEN { INPUT {file-name-1} . . .
        { OUTPUT {file-name-2} . . .
        { [ALLOWING
        {    { NO OTHERS
        {    { READERS
        {    { WRITERS                    } . . .
        {    { UPDATERS
        {    { ALL        ]
        { I-O {file-name-3} . . .
        { EXTEND {file-name-4} . . .
```

```
W OPEN  {OUTPUT {file-name-1 [WITH NO REWIND]} . . .}
        {EXTEND {file-name-2} . . .                  } . . .

PERFORM [procedure-name-1 [{THROUGH} procedure-name-2]]
                          [{THRU   }                 ]

    [imperative-statement-1 END-PERFORM]

    PERFORM [procedure-name-1 [{THROUGH} procedure-name-2]]
                              [{THRU   }                 ]

        {identifier-1}  TIMES  [imperative-statement-1 END-PERFORM]
        {integer-1   }

    PERFORM [procedure-name-1 [{THROUGH} procedure-name-2]]
                              [{THRU   }                 ]

        [WITH TEST {BEFORE}] UNTIL condition-1
        [          {AFTER }]

        [imperative-statement-1 END-PERFORM]

    PERFORM [procedure-name-1 [{THROUGH} procedure-name-2]]
                              [{THRU   }                 ]

        [WITH TEST {BEFORE}]
        [          {AFTER }]

        VARYING {identifier-2} FROM {identifier-3}
                {index-name-1}      {index-name-2}
                                    {literal-1   }
```

```
     BY {identifier-4}   UNTIL condition-1
        {literal-2   }

  [ AFTER {identifier-5  }  FROM {identifier-6  }
  [       {index-name-3  }       {index-name-4  }
  [                              {literal-3     }

     BY {identifier-7}   UNTIL condition-2 ] ...
        {literal-4   }                     ]

  [imperative-statement-1 END-PERFORM]

    PURGE cd-name-1
SRI READ file-name-1 [NEXT] RECORD [INTO identifier-1]
      [ REGARDLESS OF LOCK                 ]
      [                                    ]
      [            {UPDATERS }             ]
      [ ALLOWING   {READERS  }             ]
      [            {NO OTHERS}             ]
  [AT END imperative-statement-1]
  [NOT AT END imperative-statement-2]
  [END-READ]
 R READ file-name-1 RECORD [INTO identifier-1]
```

```
  [ REGARDLESS OF LOCK                        ]
  [                                           ]
  [           { UPDATERS  }                   ]
  [ ALLOWING  { READERS   }                   ]
  [           { NO OTHERS }                   ]

  [INVALID KEY imperative-statement-3]
  [NOT INVALID KEY imperative-statement-4]
  [END-READ]
I READ file-name-1 RECORD  [INTO identifier-1]
  [KEY IS data-name-1]
  [INVALID KEY imperative-statement-3]
  [NOT INVALID KEY imperative-statement-4]
  [END-READ]
READY [realm-name] . . .
  [                  { { CONCURRENT } [ { RETRIEVAL } ] }  ]
  [                  { { EXCLUSIVE  } [ { UPDATE    } ] }  ]
  [                  { { PROTECTED  }                   }  ]
  [                  { { BATCH      }                   }  ]
  [ USAGE-MODE IS    {                                  }  ]
  [                  {               [ { CONCURRENT } ] }  ]
  [                  { { RETRIEVAL } [ { EXCLUSIVE  } ] }  ]
  [                  { { UPDATE    } [ { PROTECTED  } ] }  ]
  [                  {               [ { BATCH      } ] }  ]
[WITH WAIT]
[ON ERROR imperative statement-1]
[NOT ON ERROR imperative statement-2]
[END-READY]
```

```
RECEIVE cd-name-1 {MESSAGE} INTO identifier-1
                  {SEGMENT}
    [NO DATA imperative-statement-1]
    [WITH DATA imperative-statement-2]
    [END-RECEIVE]

RECONNECT [record-name] WITHIN {{set-name} ...}
                               {ALL          }

    [RETAINING [{| REALM                  |}] CURRENCY]
    [          [{| RECORD                 |}]         ]
    [          [{|{SET [set-name] ...   }|}]          ]
    [          [{|{{set-name} ...       }|}]          ]
    [ON ERROR stment]
    [NOT ON ERROR stment2]
    [END-RECONNECT]
RELEASE record-name-1   [FROM identifier-1]
RETURN file-name-1 RECORD   [INTO identifier-1]
    AT END imperative-statement-1
    [NOT AT END imperative-statement-2]
    [END-RETURN]
S  REWRITE record-name-1   [FROM identifier-1]
RI REWRITE record-name-1   [FROM identifier-1]
    [ALLOWING NO OTHERS]
    [INVALID KEY imperative-statement-1]
```

```
    [NOT INVALID KEY imperative-statement-2]
    [END-REWRITE]
ROLLBACK
    [ON ERROR stment]
    [NOT ON ERROR stment2]
    [END-ROLLBACK]

SEARCH identifier-1 [VARYING {identifier-2 | index-name-1}]
    [AT END imperative-statement-1]
    {WHEN condition-1 {imperative-statement-2 | NEXT SENTENCE}} ...
    [END-SEARCH]

SEARCH ALL identifier-1  [AT END imperative-statement-1]
    WHEN {data-name-1 {IS EQUAL TO | IS =} {identifier-3 | literal-1 | arithmetic-expression-1}
         | condition-name-1}
      [AND {data-name-2 {IS EQUAL TO | IS =} {identifier-4 | literal-2 | arithmetic-expression-2}
           | condition-name-2}] ...
```

```
    { imperative-statement-2 }
    { NEXT SENTENCE          }
 [END-SEARCH]
SEND cd-name-1 FROM identifier-1

                                       { WITH identifier-2 }
SEND cd-name-1 [FROM identifier-1]     { WITH ESI          }
                                       { WITH EMI          }
                                       { WITH EGI          }

   [                          { { identifier-3 } [ LINE  ] } ]
   [ { BEFORE }  ADVANCING    { { integer-1    } [ LINES ] } ]
   [ { AFTER  }               { { mnemonic-name-1 }        } ]
   [                          { { PAGE            }        } ]
 [REPLACING LINE]

                                   { index-name-2 }
SET { index-name-1 } ...       TO  { identifier-2 }
    { identifier-1 }               { integer-1    }

SET {index-name-3} ...  { UP BY   }  { identifier-3 }
                        { DOWN BY }  { integer-2    }

SET { {mnemonic-name-1} ... TO { ON  } } ...
                               { OFF }
```

```
SET {condition-name-1} ... TO TRUE

SET pointer-id TO REFERENCE OF identifier

SET status-code-id TO {SUCCESS}
                      {FAILURE}

                                       {identifier              }
SET {identifier            }  TO       {ADDRESS OF identifier   }
    {ADDRESS OF identifier }           {NULL                    }
                                       {NULLS                   }

SORT file-name-1 {ON {ASCENDING } KEY {data-name-1} ...} ...
                     {DESCENDING}

    [WITH DUPLICATES IN ORDER]
    [COLLATING SEQUENCE IS alphabet-name-1]

     {INPUT PROCEDURE IS procedure-name-1 [{THROUGH} procedure-name-2]}
     {                                     {THRU   }                  }
     {USING {file-name-2} ...                                         }

     {OUTPUT PROCEDURE IS procedure-name-3 [{THROUGH} procedure-name-4]}
     {                                      {THRU   }                  }
     {GIVING {file-name-3} ...                                         }
```

```
START file-name-1 [ KEY { IS EQUAL TO                          } data-name-1 ]
                        { IS =                                 }
                        { IS GREATER THAN                      }
                        { IS >                                 }
                        { IS NOT LESS THAN                     }
                        { IS NOT <                             }
                        { IS GREATER THAN OR EQUAL TO          }
                        { IS >=                                }

        [ REGARDLESS OF LOCK                ]
        [                                   ]
        [ ALLOWING { UPDATERS  }            ]
        [          { READERS   }            ]
        [          { NO OTHERS }            ]

    [INVALID KEY imperative-statement-1]
    [NOT INVALID KEY imperative-statement-2]
    [END-START]

STOP { RUN       }
     { literal-1 }

STORE record-name [[NEXT TO] DBKEY] [WITHIN {realm-name} ... ]

    [ RETAINING [ { | REALM                      | } ] CURRENCY ]
    [           [ { | RECORD                     | } ]          ]
    [           [ { | { SET [set-name] ... }     | } ]          ]
    [           [ { | { {set-name} ...     }     | } ]          ]
```

```
        [ON ERROR stment]
        [NOT ON ERROR stment2]
        [END-STORE]

STRING {{identifier-1} ... DELIMITED BY {identifier-2}} ...
       {{literal-1   }                  {literal-2   }}
                                        {SIZE        }

    INTO identifier-3
    [WITH POINTER identifier-4]
    [ON OVERFLOW imperative-statement-1]
    [NOT ON OVERFLOW imperative-statement-2]
    [END-STRING]

SUBTRACT {identifier-1} ... FROM {identifier-3 [ROUNDED]} ...
         {literal-1   }

    [ON SIZE ERROR imperative-statement-1]
    [NOT ON SIZE ERROR imperative-statement-2]
    [END-SUBTRACT]

SUBTRACT {identifier-1} ... FROM {identifier-2}
         {literal-1   }          {literal-2   }

    GIVING {identifier-3 [ROUNDED]} ...
    [ON SIZE ERROR imperative-statement-1]
    [NOT ON SIZE ERROR imperative-statement-2]
    [END-SUBTRACT]
```

```
SUBTRACT {CORRESPONDING} identifier-1 FROM identifier-2 [ROUNDED]
         {CORR         }
    [ON SIZE ERROR imperative-statement-1]
    [NOT ON SIZE ERROR imperative-statement-2]
    [END-SUBTRACT]
SUPPRESS PRINTING
TERMINATE {report-name-1} . . .
UNLOCK file-name [RECORD     ]
                 [ALL RECORDS]
UNSTRING identifier-1
    [DELIMITED BY [ALL] {identifier-2} [OR [ALL] {identifier-3}] . . . ]
                        {literal-1   }           {literal-2   }
    INTO {identifier-4 [DELIMITER IN identifier-5] [COUNT IN identifier-6]} . . .
    [WITH POINTER identifier-7]
    [TALLYING IN identifier-8]
    [ON OVERFLOW imperative-statement-1]
    [NOT ON OVERFLOW imperative-statement-2]
    [END-UNSTRING]
                                                            {{file-name-1} . . .}
                                                            {INPUT              }
USE [GLOBAL] AFTER STANDARD {EXCEPTION} PROCEDURE ON        {OUTPUT             }
                            {ERROR    }                     {I-O                }
                                                            {EXTEND             }
```

```
USE [GLOBAL] AFTER STANDARD { BEGINNING }
                            { END       }

    { FILE }                        { file-name }
    { REEL } LABEL PROCEDURE ON     { INPUT     }
    { UNIT }                        { OUTPUT    }
                                    { I-O       }
                                    { EXTEND    }
```

```
USE [GLOBAL] BEFORE REPORTING identifier-1
```

```
                            { cd-name-1                               }
                            { [ALL REFERENCES OF] identifier-1        }
USE FOR DEBUGGING ON        { file-name-1                             } ...
                            { procedure-name-1                        }
                            { ALL PROCEDURES                          }
```

```
USE [GLOBAL] FOR DB-EXCEPTION
      [ ON { {DBM$__exception-condition} ... } ]
      [    { OTHER                           } ]
```

```
S WRITE record-name-1  [FROM identifier-1]
    [ALLOWING NO OTHERS]
```

```
[ {BEFORE}  ADVANCING  { {identifier-2}  [LINE ] } ]
[ {AFTER }             { {integer-1   }  [LINES] } ]
[                      { {mnemonic-name-1}       } ]
[                      { {PAGE           }       } ]
[AT {END-OF-PAGE} imperative-statement-1]
[   {EOP        }                       ]
[NOT AT {END-OF-PAGE} imperative-statement-2]
[       {EOP        }                       ]
[END-WRITE]
```

```
RI WRITE record-name-1   [FROM identifier-1]
   [ALLOWING NO OTHERS]
   [INVALID KEY imperative-statement-1]
   [NOT INVALID KEY imperative-statement-2]
   [END-WRITE]
```

General Format for Copy and Replace Statements

```
COPY text-name-1  [ {OF} library-name-1 ]
                  [ {IN}                ]
```

```
[REPLACING {{==pseudo-text-1==   }  BY  {==pseudo-text-2==}}      ]
[          {{identifier-1         }      {identifier-2     }}      ]
[          {{literal-1            }      {literal-2        }} . . .]
[          {{word-1               }      {word-2           }}      ]

COPY record-name FROM DICTIONARY

    [REPLACING                                                        ]
    [{{==pseudo-text-1==}       {==pseudo-text-2==}}                  ]
    [{{identifier-1     }  BY   {identifier-2     }}                  ]
    [{{literal-1        }       {literal-2        }} . . .            ].
    [{{word-1           }       {word-2           }}                  ]

REPLACE   {==pseudo-text-1==   BY   ==pseudo-text-2==} . . .
REPLACE OFF
```

General Format for Conditions

RELATION CONDITION

```
{identifier-1            }  IS [NOT] GREATER THAN              {identifier-2            }
{literal-1               }  IS [NOT] >                         {literal-2               }
{arithmetic-expression-1 }  IS [NOT] LESS THAN                 {arithmetic-expression-2 }
{index-name-1            }  IS [NOT] <                         {index-name-2            }
                            IS [NOT] EQUAL TO
                            IS [NOT] =
                            IS GREATER THAN OR EQUAL TO
                            IS >=
                            IS LESS THAN OR EQUAL TO
                            IS <=
```

CLASS CONDITION

```
                        {NUMERIC         }
                        {ALPHABETIC      }
identifier-1 IS [NOT]   {ALPHABETIC-LOWER}
                        {ALPHABETIC-UPPER}
                        {class-name      }
```

CONDITION-NAME CONDITION

condition-name-1

CURRENCY INDICATOR ACCESS

```
CURRENT [ WITHIN { record-name
                   set-name
                   realm-name } ]
```

KEEPLIST ACCESS

```
{ OFFSET integer-exp
  FIRST
  LAST               } WITHIN keeplist-name
```

SWITCH-STATUS CONDITION

condition-name-1

SIGN CONDITION

```
arithmetic-expression-1 IS [NOT] { POSITIVE
                                   NEGATIVE
                                   ZERO     }
```

TENANCY CONDITION

```
[NOT] [set-name] { OWNER
                   MEMBER
                   TENANT }
```

DATABASE KEY CONDITION

```
database-key IS [NOT] { ALSO database-key
                        NULL
                        WITHIN keeplist-name }
```

SUCCESS/FAILURE CONDITION

status-code-id IS { SUCCESS | FAILURE }

NEGATED CONDITION

NOT condition-1

COMBINED CONDITION

condition-1 { { AND | OR } condition-2 } . . .

ABBREVIATED COMBINED RELATION CONDITION

relation-condition { { AND | OR } [NOT] [relational-operator] object } . . .

DATABASE KEY IDENTIFIER ACCESS

database-key-identifier

DATABASE SET OWNER ACCESS

OWNER WITHIN set-namc

RECORD SEARCH ACCESS

```
⎧ FIRST                    ⎫
⎪ LAST                     ⎪
⎪ NEXT                     ⎪
⎨ PRIOR                    ⎬
⎪ ANY                      ⎪
⎪ DUPLICATE                ⎪
⎩ [RELATIVE]   int-exp     ⎭
```

```
[record-name] [WITHIN {realm-name}] [USING [record-key] ...         ]
              [       {set-name  }] [WHERE [boolean-expression]     ]
```

boolean-express:

{boolean-alt [OR boolean-alt] . . .}

boolean-alt:

{simple-boolean-relation [AND simple-boolean-relation] . . .}

simple-boolean-relation:

```
{ boolean-condition      }
{ NOT boolean-expression }
```

boolean-condition:

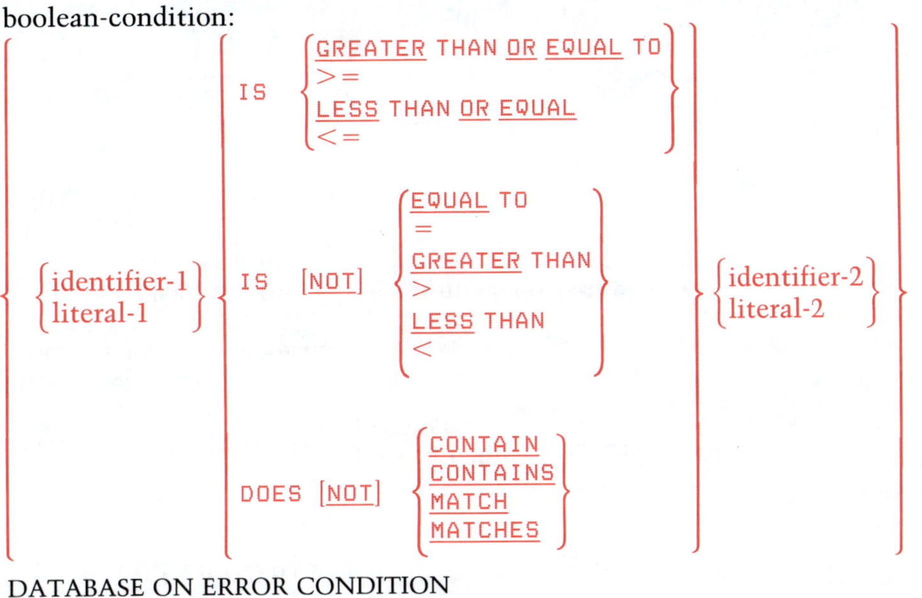

DATABASE ON ERROR CONDITION

[NOT] ON ERROR imperative statement

RETAINING CLAUSE

[RETAINING [{ | REALM | RECORD | { SET [set-name] . . . | {set-name} . . . } | }] CURRENCY]

Qualification

FORMAT 1

{ data-name-1 | condition-name } { { { IN | OF } data-name-2 } . . . [{ IN | OF } { file-name | cd-name }] | { IN | OF } { file-name | cd-name } }

FORMAT 2

paragraph-name { IN | OF } section-name

FORMAT 3

text-name { IN | OF } library-name

FORMAT 4

<u>LINAGE-COUNTER</u> { <u>IN</u> / <u>OF</u> } report-name

FORMAT 5

{ <u>PAGE-COUNTER</u> / <u>LINE-COUNTER</u> } { <u>IN</u> / <u>OF</u> } report-name

FORMAT 6

data-name-3 { { <u>IN</u> / <u>OF</u> } data-name-4 [{ <u>IN</u> / <u>OF</u> } report-name] / { <u>IN</u> / <u>OF</u> } report-name }

Miscellaneous Formats

SUBSCRIPTING

{ condition-name-1 / data-name-1 } ({ integer-1 / data-name-2 [{±} integer-2] / index-name-1 [{±} integer-3] / arithmetic-expression } . . .)

REFERENCE MODIFICATION

data-name-1 (leftmost-character-position: [length])

IDENTIFIER

```
data-name-1   [ { IN } data-name-2 ] ...   [ { IN } { cd-name     } ]
                { OF }                        { OF } { file-name   }
                                                     { report-name }

    [({subscript} . . .) ]   [(leftmost-character-position: [length])]
```

General Format for Nested Source Programs

```
IDENTIFICATION DIVISION.
PROGRAM-ID.  program-name-1  [IS INITIAL PROGRAM].
[ENVIRONMENT DIVISION.  environment-division-content]
[DATA DIVISION.  data-division-content]
[PROCEDURE DIVISION.  procedure-division-content]
[[nested-source-program] . . .
 END PROGRAM program-name-1.]
```

General Format for Nested-Source-Program

```
IDENTIFICATION DIVISION.
PROGRAM-ID.   program-name-2   [IS {COMMON | INITIAL} PROGRAM].
[ENVIRONMENT DIVISION.   environment-division-content]
[DATA DIVISION.   data-division-content]
[PROCEDURE DIVISION.   procedure-division-content]
[nested-source-program] . . .
END PROGRAM program-name-2.
```

General Format for a Sequence of Source Programs

```
{IDENTIFICATION DIVISION.
 PROGRAM-ID.   program-name-3   [IS INITIAL PROGRAM].
[ENVIRONMENT DIVISION.   environment-division-content]
[DATA DIVISION.   data-division-content]
[PROCEDURE DIVISION.   procedure-division-content]
[nested-source-program] . . .
 END PROGRAM program-name-3.} . . .
 IDENTIFICATION DIVISION.
 PROGRAM-ID.   program-name-4   [IS INITIAL PROGRAM].
[ENVIRONMENT DIVISION.   environment-division-content]
```

[DATA DIVISION. data-division-content]
[PROCEDURE DIVISION. procedure-division-content]
[[nested-source-program] . . .
END PROGRAM program-name-4.]

IV. FUNCTION NAMES AVAILABLE IN EXTENSIONS TO COBOL 85

ABS
ACOS
ANNUITY
ASIN
ATAN
CHAR
CHAR-NATIONAL
COS
CURRENT-DATE
DATE-OF-INTEGER
DAY-OF-INTEGER
DISPLAY-OF
EXCEPTION-FILE
EXCEPTION-LOCATION
EXCEPTION-STATEMENT
EXCEPTION-STATUS
EXP
FACTORIAL
FRACTION-PART
INTEGER
INTEGER-OF-DATE
INTEGER-OF-DAY
INTEGER-PART
LENGTH
LENGTH-AN
LOG
LOG10
LOWER-CASE
MAX
MEAN
MEDIAN
MIDRANGE
MIN
MOD
NATIONAL-OF
NUMVAL
NUMVAL-C
ORD
ORD-MAX
ORD-MIN
PI
PRESENT-VALUE
RANDOM
RANGE
REM
REVERSE
SIGN
SIN
SQRT
STANDARD-DEVIATION
SUM
TAN
UPPER-CASE
VARIANCE
WHEN-COMPILED

V. NEW COBOL 9X RESERVED WORDS

ALIGN
B-AND
B-NOT
B-OR
B-XOR
CLASS-ID
CONFORMING
END-INVOKE
EXCEPTION-OBJECT
FACTORY
FUNCTION
INHERITS
INTERFACE
INTERFACE-ID
INVARIANT
INVOKE
METHOD
METHOD-ID
NATIONAL
NATIONAL-EDITED
OBJECT
OVERRIDE
PROPERTY
RAISE
REPOSITORY
RESERVED
RETURNING
REUSES
SELF
SUPER
SYSTEM-OBJECT
UNIVERSAL